7 STEPS TO REMOVING SPYWARE

Get Rid of Threats & Improve

your Digital Hygiene

Nick Laughter

7 STEPS TO REMOVING SPYWARE

Disclaimer: It is recommended to take a full backup of your computer before running any cleanup utilities. By using this information you agree that I am not responsible for any real or perceived damage to your computer or loss of data. Use at your own risk.

For information contact: Spyware Jedi
www.spywarejedi.com

ISBN: 978-1-329-54204-4

First Edition: September 2015

INTRODUCTION

Is your computer running slow? Do you have spyware or viruses that seem impossible to remove? This book can help guide you through cleaning up your PC and get it running like the day you bought it. With over 7 years of experience as an IT Professional, I have found the best (free and easy) cleanup tools on the web. Why take your computer to a repair shop and pay $100, $200, or even $300+ when you can remove these threats yourself? Our step-by-step guide makes it easy to eliminate spyware, malware, adware, rootkits and viruses in about 1-2 hours.

In addition, you will learn how to boost your PC's performance and improve Digital Hygiene. Digital Hygiene is a term used to describe the cleanliness or uncleanliness of one's digital habitat. This could be used to describe one's desktop icons, file structure, folder trees, Photoshop files or hard drive, Facebook page or digital persona."

- cyborganthropology

BEFORE YOU BEGIN

Make sure to read these cleanup instructions carefully. Each of the recommended tools are powerful and do a great job removing threats, however they can also damage your machine if not used properly.

Often times spyware / viruses make it hard to browse the web and grab the tools required for removal. It can be frustrating when you get redirected to other websites, or try and close down annoying pop-up windows with little to no success.

Don't worry, there is a solution! The best thing to do in this situation is go to another PC (which is not infected), plug in a flash drive, and save the installers to it. Then you can bring the flash drive over to the infected machine and run them successfully.

Note: You can save an installer to the flash drive by doing the following: When you hit download on a program, select the "Save As" option, navigate to your flash drive, and save the (.exe) file there.

CONTENTS

STEPS 1-7

Spyware Cleanup Guide & Tools

Download & Run | RogueKiller

www.spywarejedi.com/downloads/roguekiller.exe

- If you are using Internet Explorer then choose the option to "Save As", then select your Desktop folder and hit "Save". If you are using Google Chrome, then the installer will save to your "Downloads" folder by default.

- Next, right click on the "roguekiller.exe" icon and choose "Properties", then check the box next to "Unblock" (towards the bottom) and hit "Ok". If you don't see this option simply hit "Ok".

- Now double click the program to run it. First, it will run through a "Pre-scan" to find and kill any threats currently running on your machine.

- When the Pre-scan has finished, then click on the "Scan" button (top right). Once the primary scan has completed, click on the "Registry" tab, right click any one of the registry items, and hit "Select all".

- Lastly, click the "Delete" option (right-hand menu) and wait for the status bar at the top to say "Items Deleted Successfully" and then close down the program.

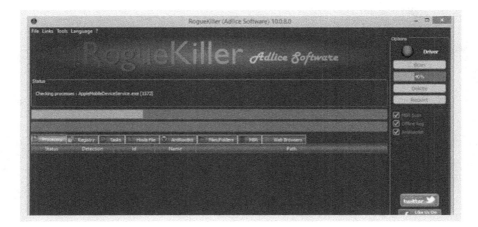

Step 2

Download & Run | ComboFix

www.spywarejedi.com/downloads/combofix.exe

- If you are using Internet Explorer then choose the option to "Save As", then select your Desktop folder and hit "Save". If you are using Google Chrome, then the installer will save to your "Downloads" folder by default.

- Next, right click on the "combofix.exe" icon and choose "Properties", then check the box next to "Unblock" (towards the bottom) and hit "Ok". If you don't see this option simply hit "Ok".

- Then double click it to run the program. Follow the installation wizard and click "Next", "Next", "Yes", etc. through all the

prompt boxes. It will start scanning your
computer and go through all of its stages.

- Once it reaches the end of the scan it may
  reboot your computer automatically (this is
  normal). ComboFix will pull up a text
  window with the results once it has
  completed successfully.

```
C:\  .                                                          - □ |
:\Program Files\MyWebSearch\bar\Notifier\MAID.F3S
:\Program Files\MyWebSearch\bar\Notifier\MAILBOX.F3S
:\Program Files\MyWebSearch\bar\Notifier\OPERA.F3S
:\Program Files\MyWebSearch\bar\Notifier\ROBOT.F3S
:\Program Files\MyWebSearch\bar\Notifier\SEDUCT.F3S
:\Program Files\MyWebSearch\bar\Notifier\SURFER.F3S
:\Program Files\MyWebSearch\bar\Settings\prevcfg2.htm
:\Program Files\MyWebSearch\bar\Settings\s_pid.dat
:\Program Files\MyWebSearch\bar\Settings\setting2.htm
:\Program Files\MyWebSearch\bar\Settings\settings.dat
:\Program Files\PersonalSec\psecurity.exe
:\WINDOWS\awihalafunaner.dll
:\WINDOWS\casemx.dll
:\WINDOWS\system32\f3PSSavr.scr
:\WINDOWS\system32\inunideb.ini
:\WINDOWS\system32\win32extension.dll

eleting Folders:

:\Documents and Settings\Administrator\Local Settings\Application Data\(314EEFE
-2384-4B5E-A940-DABB28DA05DC)
:\Program Files\FunWebProducts
:\Program Files\MyWebSearch
:\Program Files\PersonalSec
```

Download & Run | AdwCleaner

www.spywarejedi.com/downloads/adwcleaner.exe

- If you are using Internet Explorer then choose the option to "Save As", then select your Desktop folder and hit "Save". If you are using Google Chrome, then the installer will save to your "Downloads" folder by default.

- Next, right click on the "adwcleaner.exe" icon and choose "Properties", then check the box next to "Unblock" (towards the bottom) and hit "Ok". If you don't see this option simply hit "Ok".

- Then double click it to run the program. Click on "Scan", then once the scan has completed select "Clean".

- Click through the prompt boxes, "Yes", "Next", etc. and then the program will ask to reboot to complete thoroughly, this is fine click "Ok" on this and let it reboot your computer.

- AdwCleaner will pull up a text window with the results once it has completed successfully.

Step 4

Download & Run | Junkware Removal Tool

www.spywarejedi.com/downloads/jrt.exe

- If you are using Internet Explorer then choose the option to "Save As", then select your Desktop folder and hit "Save". If you are using Google Chrome, then the installer will save to your "Downloads" folder by default.

- Next, right click on the "jrt.exe" icon and choose "Properties", then check the box next to "Unblock" (towards the bottom) and hit "Ok". If you don't see this option simply hit "Ok".

- Then double click it to run the program. Follow the installation wizard and click "any key to continue". It will start scanning your computer and go through all of its stages.

- Once it reaches the end of the scan and completes successfully, it will pull up a text window with the results. Close down window when you have finished viewing the report.

Download & Run | Malwarebytes

www.spywarejedi.com/downloads/malwarebytes.exe

- If you are using Internet Explorer then choose the option "Run" to start installing. If you are using Google Chrome, then the installer will save to your "Downloads" folder by default, and then double click to install.

- Follow the installation wizard and click "Next", "Next", "Yes", etc. through all the prompt boxes. Click "Update now" on the Database section to get the latest definitions. Then click "Scan now" and let Malwarebytes scan your computer.

- Once it reaches the end of the scan, if it finds any threats it will ask you to apply actions

(Quarantine or Delete) and click "Apply". It may prompt you to reboot your computer if major threats are found. This is normal so go ahead and delete the threats and reboot.

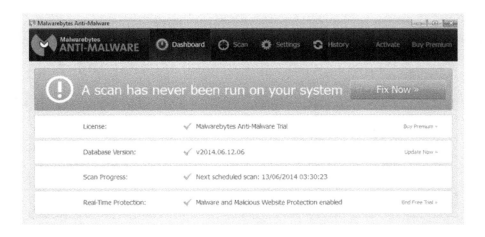

Step 6

Reset Browser Settings:

- Open up Internet Explorer, click on the "Tools" icon (gear image located on top right) then select "Internet Options". Click on the "Advanced" tab, then click the "Reset" button. Check the box next to "Delete personal settings" and hit "Reset".

- Once default settings have been restored, click "Ok", "Apply", etc. and close down all browser windows for these new changes to take effect.

Reset Internet Explorer Settings   ⊠   ?   ×

⚠ **Are you sure you want to reset all Internet Explorer settings?**   Programs | Advanced

Resetting includes doing the following:

- Disabling toolbars and add-ons
- Deleting temporary internet files, webpage history, cookies, web form information, and passwords
- Resetting default web browser settings, search providers, and home pages

Resetting does not affect:

- Favorites and feeds, Internet connection settings, Group Policy settings, and Content Advisor settings

You must restart Internet Explorer for these changes to take effect.

How does resetting affect my computer?   Reset   Cancel

endering*

and tabs
changes

ws and tabs
abs

es
rites*

Step 7

Remove Unwanted Programs

- Click on "Start" menu, select "Control Panel", change View By: category (on top right) to either "Large or Small icons", and then click on "Programs & Features". Note: For Windows 8 / 8.1 / 10 users you will need to right-click on the start menu to get to the Control Panel.

- Right click on any suspicious or unwanted programs and select "Uninstall". Reboot your computer if the uninstall process calls for it.

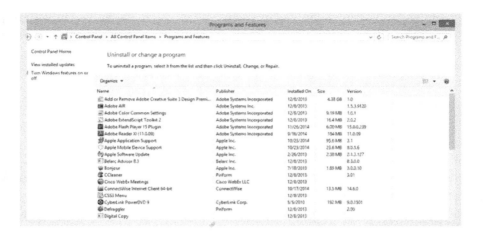

ADDITIONAL TIPS

For Advanced Users Only

Run Command: sfc /scannow

- Click on the "Start" menu, type in "cmd", then right click on (CMD) and choose "Run as administrator". In the command prompt box type in "sfc /scannow" and press "Enter".

- Wait for scan to find and fix any damaged system files, and then close down the command prompt when it's finished.

Download & Run | HiJack This

- Go to [www.spywarejedi.com/downloads] to download the latest release. Once you've downloaded "Hijack This" to your computer, then double click it to run the program.

- Follow the installation wizard and click "Next", "Next", "Yes", etc. through all the prompt boxes. Then select "Do a system scan only" or "Scan" and wait for the scan to complete.

- Put a checkmark next to any R0, R1, DPF, URL Redirection and Scheduled Task line items, then hit "Fixed checked". Close the program when finished.

Download & Run | cCleaner

- Go to [www.spywarejedi.com/downloads] to download the latest release. Once you've downloaded "cCleaner" to your computer, then double click it to run the program.

- Follow the installation wizard and click "Next", "Next", "Yes", etc. through all the prompt boxes.

- Then click on the "Cleaner" tab, hit "Analyze" and wait for results to populate. Once all items display then hit "Run Cleaner". Repeat this process a few times until it wipes out all temp files, cookies, history, etc.

- Then click on the "Registry" tab and hit "Scan for issues". Once it finds all broken registry keys hit "Fix selected issues". It will ask you if you want to backup changes to the Registry, click "No" and then hit the "Fix All Selected Issues" option. Repeat this process until no more broken registry keys populate in the results box.

- Finally, click the "X" on the top right to close down the program.

Remove Unwanted Startup Items

- Click on the "Start" menu, type in "Regedit" and hit "Enter". Navigate to the HKEY_Local_Machine / Microsoft / Windows / CurrentVersion / "Run" & "Runonce" folders. Remove all unwanted startup tasks within these subfolders by right clicking the undesired task or program, and choosing "Delete".

- Repeat these same steps under: HKEY_Current_User / Microsoft / Windows / CurrentVersion / "Run" & "Runonce" folders as well. Then close down the Registry window when finished and reboot your computer.

- You can remove any remaining items by going to "Start" -> "All Programs" -> "Startup" folder and then deleting unwanted startup items from this location as well.

Booting info Safe Mode

- If you are unable to browse the internet, or utilize the removal tools in normal mode, try running them in "Safe Mode with Networking". To do this, simply restart your computer, press "F8" repeatedly after the boot screen. The boot screen displays the option "Press F2 or F12 to enter setup".

- Then select the option "Safe Mode with Networking" and press "Enter". Log into any user profile with administrative rights and then run your cleanup programs.

Run a CheckDisk

- Try running a CheckDisk which can help find and fix corrupt system files / broken registry keys. This can be done by right clicking on "My Computer" & choosing "Properties", then select "Error Checking". Check the box next to "Fix and detect errors", then reboot the computer.

Additional Tools & Utilities

- Some other helpful antivirus and antispyware tools include: (Microsoft Security Essentials, AVG, GMER, Root Repeal, rKill, TDSSKiller, Spybot, and Super AntiSpyware).

- Most of these tools can be found at www.download.com, www.bleepingcomputer.com or by doing a quick Google search.

Re-install the Operating System

- Lastly, if you have tried all of the steps listed above and your computer is still acting up, you may need to take a full backup of your hard drive, then wipe and re-install the operating system.

- I recommend using Macrium Reflect (free) to take a full image backup of your hard drive,

then use the re-installation disk provided
when you bought your computer.

- Then once you have your Operating System
  loaded up / activated you can copy your files
  (Documents, Pictures, Videos, etc.) back
  over.

COMPUTER MAINTENANCE

Daily, Weekly, and Monthly Tasks

Daily Tasks:

- Reboot computer every day.
- Backup data and important documents.
- Update Antispyware & Antivirus programs.

Weekly Tasks

- Cleanup temp files and broken registry keys with cCleaner.
- Update Antispyware & Antivirus programs.

Monthly Tasks

- Run "Defraggler" to compress fragmented files on your hard drive.
- Run your antivirus / antispyware programs to find and remove threats.
- Install important Windows Updates and security patches.
- Un-install any unwanted programs from your PC.

Both "cCleaner" and "Defraggler" can be downloaded at www.piriform.com

F A Q ' s

How did I get spyware & viruses?

Spyware comes from the internet and/or programs that are downloaded from the web. Spyware/Viruses originate from computer programmers in the world that make their living by tracking who you are, what sites you go to, personal information (such as birth date, social security number and financial information). Spyware/Viruses can come from a variety of places on the internet. These include: phony media downloads, pirated music & videos, ad's, spam sites, and email attachments.

How do I avoid spyware?

Avoid suspicious websites (including: spam, pornographic, and torrent websites). Use caution when clicking on links to other websites. Check the source of emails and attachments. Don't download free or pirated music, videos or games. Stay away from ads and social engineering attacks. Install only trusted and/or purchased software.

How do I remove spyware & viruses?

The first step to removing spyware/viruses is to boot your computer into Safe Mode. Followed by running a variety of antivirus/antispyware programs. Make sure to remove all temp files and remove unwanted registry startup tasks. For step-by-step instructions see pages 2-8 of this book or visit www.spywarejedi.com.

How do I improve my computer's performance?
Remove temp files and clean broken registry keys with cCleaner. Then remove any spyware using the following programs (Malwarebytes, Spybot, & Microsoft Security Essentials). Defrag your computer's C: drive using Defraggler. Check your computer's currently installed RAM using Crucial Scan. You may be able to add more memory to your machine, which can drastically improve performance and speed.

What are good computer maintenance tips?
Reboot your computer every day. Make sure to backup important data (documents, pictures, videos, financial info, etc). Run cCleaner to remove temp files, clean registry and empty

recycle bin. Update/run antivirus & antispyware programs to check for infections. Remove any found threats and reboot computer if necessary. Remove any un-wanted or un-used programs from Add/Remove programs inside of Control Panel.

What are the best programs?

Top Antivirus Programs – (Microsoft Security Essentials, AVG, and ComboFix). Top Antispyware Programs – (Malwarebytes, RogueKiller, AdwCleaner, Spybot, and SuperAntiSpyware).

What is the difference between spyware & a virus?

Spyware/Malware can have a variety of effects: It can steal your personal information (identity theft). Also, floods your web browser with pop-up advertising, keystroke-logging, slows down internet connection, hijacks your browser and redirects to other URL's. It can also cause programs to freeze up and crash your computer.

A virus trys to infect a computer and replicate. It's main goal is to infect as many computers as possible and as fast as possible. When you accidentally install a virus, the malicious code that is the virus tries to find ways to use your PC to infect other machines. Viruses can cause you to loose important data and damage your computer.

HELPFUL SITES

Related Websites & Links

AntiSpyware / Antivirus

The following tools (AdwCleaner, ComboFix, Rkill, Malwarebytes, RogueKiller, Junkware Removal Tool, and HiJack This) can all be found at:

- www.spywarejedi.com
- www.bleepingcomputer.com

Cleanup / Repair / Performance

The following tools (cCleaner and Defraggler) can

both be found at:

- www.piriform.com

How To's / Instructions / Guides

Visit Spyware Jedi and Helpdesk Jedi for more helpful information, How To's and guides:

- www.spywarejedi.com
- www.helpdeskjedi.com

About the Author

Nick Laughter is an IT Professional and Web Developer based out of Denver, CO. He has over 7+ years experience working with a wide variety of IT related issues including: networking, spyware removal, phone and vendor management, website design, coding, and more.

Thanks for reading! Please add a short review on Amazon and let me know what you thought!

www.ingramcontent.com/pod-product-compliance
Lightning Source LLC
Chambersburg PA
CBHW051217050326
40689CB00008B/1348